D1394683

THE CHINESE HOROSCOPES LIBRARY

ROOSTER

KWOK MAN-HO

DORLING KINDERSLEY
LONDON • NEW YORK • STUTTGART

A DORLING KINDERSLEY BOOK

Senior Editor Sharon Lucas
Art Editor Camilla Fox
Managing Editor Krystyna Mayer
Managing Art Editor Derek Coombes
DTP Designer Doug Miller
Production Controller Antony Heller

Artworks: Danuta Mayer 4, 8, 11, 17, 27, 29, 31, 33, 35;
Giuliano Fornari 21; Jane Thomson; Sarah Ponder.

Special Photography by Steve Gorton. Thank you to the Bristol City Museum & Art Gallery,
Oriental Section; The British Museum, Chinese Post Office, Percival David Foundation of
Chinese Art, and The Powell-Cotton Museum.

Additional Photography: Eric Crichton, Mike Dunning, Jo Foord, Philip Gatward, Steve
Gorton, Liz McAulay, Stephen Oliver, Tim Ridley, Karl Shone, Clive Streeter.

Picture Credits: Bridgeman Art Library/Oriental Museum, Durham University 19bl; Bruce
Coleman/Gerald Cubitt 20bl.

First published in Great Britain in 1994
by Dorling Kindersley Limited,
9 Henrietta Street, London WC2E 8PS

A CIP catalogue record for this book is available from the British Library

ISBN 0-7513-0125-6

Reproduced by GRB Editrice, Verona, Italy
Printed and bound in Hong Kong by Imago

CONTENTS

INTRODUCING CHINESE HOROSCOPES

For thousands of years, the Chinese have used their astrology and religion to establish a harmony between people and the world around them.

The exact origins of the twelve animals of Chinese astrology – the Rat, Ox, Tiger, Rabbit, Dragon, Snake, Horse, Ram, Monkey, Rooster, Dog, and Pig remain a mystery. Nevertheless, these animals are important in Chinese astrology. They are much more than general signposts to the year, and to the possible good or bad times ahead for us all. The twelve animals of Chinese astrology are considered to be a reflection of the Universe itself.

YIN AND YANG

The many differences in our natures, moods, health, and fortunes reflect the wider changes within the Universe. The Chinese believe that

every single thing in the Universe is held in balance by the dynamic, cosmic forces of yin and yang. Yin is feminine, watery, and cool; the force of the Moon and the rain. Yang is masculine, solid, and hot; the force of the Sun and the Earth. According to ancient Chinese belief, the concentrated essences of yin and yang became the four seasons, and the scattered essences of yin and yang became the myriad creatures that are found on Earth.

YIN AND YANG SYMBOL
White represents the female force of yin, and black represents the masculine force of yang.

The twelve animals of Chinese astrology are all associated with either yin or yang. The forces of yin rise as winter approaches. These forces decline with the warmth of spring, when yang begins to assert

itself. Even in the course of a normal day, yin and yang are at work, constantly changing and balancing. These forces also naturally rise and fall within us all.

Everyone has their own internal balance of yin and yang. This affects our tempers, ambitions, and health. We also respond to the changes of weather, to the environment, and to the people who surround us.

THE FIVE ELEMENTS

All that we can touch, taste, or see is divided into five basic types or elements – wood, fire, earth, gold, and water. Everything in the Universe can be linked to one of these elements.

For example, the element gold is linked to the Monkey and to the Rooster. This element is also linked to the colour white, acrid-tasting food, the season of autumn, and the

emotion of sorrow. The activity of these elements indicates the fortune that may befall us.

AN INDIVIDUAL DISCOVERY

Chinese astrology can help you balance your yin and yang. It can also tell you which element you are, and the colours, tastes, parts of the body, or emotions that are linked to your particular sign. Your fortune can be prophesied according to the year, month, day, and hour in which you were born. You can identify the type of people to whom you are attracted, and the career that will suit your character. You can understand your changes of mood, your reactions to other places, and to other people. In essence, you can start to discover what makes you an individual.

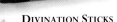

DIVINATION STICKS
Another ancient and popular method of Chinese fortune-telling is using special divination sticks to obtain a specific reading from prediction books.

CASTING YOUR HOROSCOPE

The Chinese calendar is based on the movement of the Moon, unlike the calendar used in the Western world, which is based on the movement of the Sun.

Before you begin to cast your Chinese horoscope, check your year of birth on the chart on pages 44 to 45. Check particularly carefully if you were born in the early months of the year. The Chinese year does not usually begin until January or February, and you might belong to the previous Chinese year. For example, if you were born in 1961 you might assume that you were born in the Year of the Ox. However, if your birthday falls before 15 February you belong to the previous Chinese year, which is the Year of the Rat.

THE SIXTY-YEAR CYCLE

The Chinese measure the passing of time by cycles of sixty years. The twelve astrological animals appear five times during the sixty-year cycle, and they appear in a slightly different form every time. For example, if you were born in 1969

you are a Rooster Announcing the Dawn, but if you were born in 1981, you are a Rooster in the Cage.

MONTHS, DAYS, AND HOURS

The twelve lunar months of the Chinese calendar do not correspond exactly with the twelve Western calendar months. This is because Chinese months are lunar, whereas Western months are solar. Chinese months are normally twenty-nine to thirty days long, and every three to four years an extra month is added to keep approximately in step with the Western year.

One Chinese hour is equal to two Western hours, and the twelve Chinese hours correspond to the twelve animal signs.

The year, month, day, and hour of birth are the keys to Chinese astrology. Once you know them, you can start to unlock your personal Chinese horoscope.

	Water			
	Earth	Gold		
	Wood	Yin		
	Fire	Yang		

CHINESE ASTROLOGICAL WHEEL

In the centre of the wheel is the yin and yang symbol. It is surrounded by the Chinese astrological character linked to each animal. The band of colour reveals your element, and the outer ring shows whether you are yin or yang.

· ROOSTER ·
MYTHS AND LEGENDS

*According to Chinese legend, the Jade Emperor, the ruler of
Heaven, asked to see the Earth's twelve most interesting
animals, then awarded the Rooster tenth place.*

In China, the rooster is believed to
ward off evil. A picture of a red
rooster is hung up to protect
the house from fire,
while a white rooster
placed on a coffin is
reputed to keep
demons at bay.
The rooster also
symbolizes
courage and male
vigour. It is not
eaten in China, but
there is a tradition of
rooster fighting that
continues today,
even though it is
strictly prohibited.
A crowing rooster
symbolizes great
achievement, and a
gift of a rooster with a fine comb
expresses the wish that the recipient
will be granted an official post.

ROOSTER DISH WITH PEONIES
*This ancient Chinese dish depicts a
rooster, a butterfly, and peonies, which
symbolize wealth and distinction.*

THE ROOSTER AND HIS COMB
Long ago there was a hunter who
hunted by day, and tended
his lovely garden in the
evenings. One day he
found his favourite
mulberry bush
shrivelled and
wilting. He did
all he could to
save it, but it
perished. The
hunter shouted to
the sun, "You are too
hot and have destroyed
my beautiful bush.
I am going to get
my revenge."
Taking careful aim
with his bow and
arrow, the hunter
fired at the sun, and the arrow hit
the sun straight in the eye. The sun
cried out in pain, and ran to hide

itself behind the clouds. All the animals of the kingdom urged the sun to come out again, but it stayed behind the clouds. Soon the land grew dark and cold, and the animals realized that they would die if the sun did not appear. They called a great Council, and decided to try their best to persuade the sun to come out again.

The first to volunteer to call the sun was the ox, but his voice was so deep and low that the sun could not hear it. The tiger was next, but his roared message sounded so fierce and terrifying that the sun hid even deeper into the clouds.

At last the rooster strutted into the Council. "Let me try," he said, somewhat arrogantly, and called out loud and clear. The sun heard the rooster's agreeable voice, and peered out. The rooster called again, reassuringly, and the sun came out completely, and told the rooster, "I will give you a very special comb to comb your feathers before you call me each morning."

The sun threw down the comb and the rooster ran to catch it. Unfortunately, in his excitement, the rooster mistimed the catch, and the comb landed upside down on his head, where it remains to this day.

HAN DYNASTY HEADS
These bronze rooster heads are finials, and date from China's Han dynasty.

· ROOSTER ·
PERSONALITY

The Rooster has an open and courageous nature, and will always make itself available for others in need. It enjoys, and openly indulges in, the good things in life.

You are excellent company, and usually adapt well to different circumstances. Maintaining your appearance takes up a considerable amount of your time, and you are just as critical about your own taste as you are about others'.

MOTIVATION
You enjoy the best of everything, and want your needs to be met. You expect to follow your own routine without any interference from other people.

However, there is a certain innocence in your approach, and your selfishness is never intended to

ROOSTERS AND FLOWERS
This Chinese, porcelain vessel is decorated with exquisitely painted roosters and flowers.

be hurtful. Although you are often straightforward to the point of embarrassment, this is not through vindictiveness, but because you feel that others should know the truth.

THE IMPERIAL ROOSTER
Superficially, you are charming, and rarely exhibit the true depth of your extensive knowledge. In reality, you have an independent spirit, and are wary of others. Although you possess a streak of exhibitionism, you also have a compassionate side. This altruism tends to come to the fore when others ask for your help.

You are trustworthy, and offer sensible advice, but you rarely reveal yourself to other people, and may sometimes appear to be rather off-hand and erratic.

You have a vulnerable nature, and often feel insecure, but you hide these weaknesses beneath humour and conversation. Your true nature is usually only seen by your close friends, or in times of crisis.

You are a sociable and charming romantic partner. It is difficult for you to commit yourself, but once you have, you are dependable and responsible.

As a parent, you are dedicated and organized. You can also be very protective, but always like to give yourself the freedom to enjoy life's luxuries.

THE ROOSTER CHILD

The young Rooster is open, inquisitive, and good company, but its interests may have to be subtly directed by its parents.

STANDING ROOSTER
The jaunty stance of this standing rooster suggests the natural pride and self-confidence of the Rooster personality. The figure is porcelain, and is from 18th-century China.

· ROOSTER ·
LOVE

*The Rooster is a charming creature. It loves fine clothes and
good company, and always wants to impress. Usually, it has
a trail of besotted admirers.*

You relish an element of
conquest in love. Romance
must never be easy and
predictable for you – if it is,
you are soon likely to be off in
search of a new partner.

Your independence is
vital, and life could be
difficult for a partner
who needs you to be by
their side. You are
jealous, but are careful
not to show it.

Once you feel that you
are truly involved in a
relationship, you are an
intelligent and agreeable
partner. In the security of a
committed relationship you
are willing to allow your
sensitivities to surface.

You are renowned
for your honesty, but can
sometimes appear to be
brutally off-hand.
Unintentionally, this
thoughtless behaviour could
easily hurt the one you love.

Ideally, you are suited to
the Ox and the Snake. The
Ox can offer sociability,
excitement, and the
security and comfort
that you secretly need.
The Snake shares your
love of clothes and
colour, but also
appreciates your more
subtle side.

GODDESS OF LOVE
*Kuan Yin is a powerful
figure in Chinese mythology.
Once a male Buddhist
deity, she is now known
as the goddess of mercy,
and as Sung-tzu, the
giver of children.*

CHINESE COMPATIBILITY WHEEL

Find your animal sign, then look for the animals that share its background colour – the Rooster has a yellow background, and is most compatible with the Ox and the Snake. The symbol in the centre of the wheel represents double happiness.

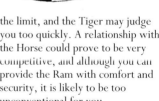

The Dragon welcomes your attention, and shares your love of performance. The Pig should be tolerant and understanding, and will ignore your boastfulness or criticisms. The Rat may prove to be a difficult partner unless you allow it to see beneath your surface.

The Tiger and the Rabbit could prove too critical – you may push the Rabbit's patience to the limit, and the Tiger may judge you too quickly. A relationship with the Horse could prove to be very competitive, and although you can provide the Ram with comfort and security, it is likely to be too unconventional for you.

Your honesty complements the Monkey's astuteness, but it could take some time to understand each other. Although a partnership with another Rooster would undoubtedly be lively, it is also likely to be full of turbulence and disagreement.

ORCHID

In China, the orchid, or Lan Hua, is an emblem of love and beauty. It is also a fertility symbol, and represents many offspring.

· ROOSTER ·
CAREER

The Rooster is intuitive, intelligent, and well organized. It does not enjoy being told what to do, and is best suited to careers with an element of independence.

TAILOR

The work of the tailor requires a combination of practical skill and creative flair. This suits the Rooster well, since it is confident, convincing, and capable, and has an eye for clothes and colour.

Sewing machine

FASHION DESIGNER

Style is of great interest to the extravagant Rooster. It loves to create anything new and different, and could derive great satisfaction from a career as a fashion designer.

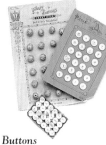

Patterns

Buttons

ENTERTAINER

The Rooster is a natural entertainer. It is relaxing company, and enjoys socializing, whatever the occasion. When entertaining, the Rooster enjoys using beautiful objects, such as this Chinese chocolate pot from the late K'ang-hsi or Yung Chen reign (c.1720–1735), and early 17th-century, Ming dynasty tea bowl.

Chinese chocolate pot

Chinese tea bowl

SERVICE WORKER

A career as a service worker suits the Rooster, because it is never afraid to accept challenges, and is rarely defeated by obstacles. It always needs to retain some independence, however.

Railway worker's whistle

Firefighter's helmet

BEAUTICIAN

The beautician's work appeals to the Rooster's flamboyance. It would adore this 19th-century Chinese, silver fingernail protector.

Beautician's bottle

Fingernail protector

19

· ROOSTER ·
HEALTH

Yin and yang are in a continual state of flux within the body. Good health is dependent upon the balance of yin and yang being constantly harmonious.

There is a natural minimum and maximum level of yin and yang in the human body. The body's energy is known as ch'i, and is a yang force. The movement of ch'i in the human body is complemented by the movement of blood, which is a yin force. The very slightest displacement of the balance of yin or yang in the human body can quickly lead to poor health and sickness. However, yang illness can be cured by yin treatment, and yin illness can be cured by yang treatment. Everybody has their own individual balance of yin and yang. It is likely that a hot-tempered person will have strong yang forces, and that a peaceful person will have strong yin forces. Your nature is closely identified with your health, and before Chinese medicine can be prescribed, your moods must be carefully taken into account. A balance of joy, anger, sadness, happiness, worry, pensiveness, and fear must always be maintained. This fine balance is known in China as the Harmony of the Seven Sentiments.

LINGCHIH FUNGUS
The fungus shown in this detail from a Ch'ing dynasty bowl is the "immortal" lingchih fungus, which symbolizes longevity.

LOTUS FLOWER
The seeds of the lotus flower are rich in vitamin C, and are combined with lily to restore ch'i.

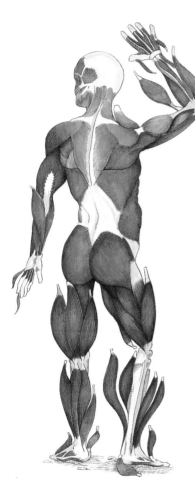

Born in the Year of the Rooster, you are associated with the element gold. This element is linked with the lungs, large intestine, nose, skin, and hair. These are the parts of the human body that are most relevant to the general pattern of your health. You are also associated with the emotion of sorrow, and with acrid-tasting food.

The lotus flower (*Nelumbo nucifera*) is associated with your astrological sign. Its seeds are used to strengthen the spleen and stomach, promote mental stability, and control the loss of body fluids.

In China, lotus seed and lily soup is served at the end of wedding banquets. This is because their Chinese names form a pun on "continuous sons" and "one hundred together", and the soup represents a wish for one hundred years of married life, with many sons.

Chinese medicine is specific, therefore never take lotus seeds or any other herb unless you are following advice from a doctor.

ASTROLOGY AND ANATOMY

Your element, gold, is associated with two major organs, the lungs and the large intestine. The lungs are yin, and the large intestine is yang.

· ROOSTER ·
LEISURE

The Rooster is a natural performer, and loves being the centre of attention. However, it also likes to escape to a private, comfortable place where it can truly relax.

EXERCISING

Morning exercise is particularly beneficial for the Rooster, because it sets it up for the energetic day ahead. Skipping and running appeal to the Rooster, because they are forms of exercise that can be done at virtually any time.

Skipping rope

Stopwatch

Training shoes

WALKING

Although walking may seem to be too tame for the highly sociable Rooster, it is a valuable pastime. Walking provides the Rooster with a relaxing escape from its usual frenetic activity.

HOME ACCOUNTING
The Rooster is extravagant with its money. Luckily, it is very well organized, and always keeps a careful eye on its spending habits.

Home accounts book and calculator

Alto saxophone

ROOSTER LOGO
The French brothers Charles and Emile Pathé set up a film company, which produced newsreels after 1909. This rooster is their company's distinctive logo.

Pathé Brothers' logo

Microphone

PERFORMING
The limelight is the Rooster's natural environment. It is a flamboyant perfomer, whatever the occasion or the company. It would thrive on the exposure provided by a solo saxophone performance, or by singing to a large cabaret audience.

· ROOSTER ·
SYMBOLISM

*Each astrological animal is linked with a certain food,
direction, colour, emotion, association, and symbol. The
Rooster is also associated with the season of autumn.*

**Chinese,
porcelain
rooster**

COLOUR
*In China, brilliant white is
the colour of purity. It is also
the colour that is linked with
the Rooster. This porcelain
blanc de chine Rooster is
from the Ch'ing dynasty.*

Cloves

FOOD
*Acrid-tasting foods, such as cloves,
are associated with the Rooster.*

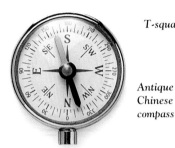

T-square

SYMBOL
The Rooster's symbol
in Chinese astrology is
the T-square.

**Antique
Chinese
compass**

DIRECTION
The Chinese compass points south,
whereas the Western compass points
north. The Rooster's direction is the west.

EMOTION
Sorrow is the emotion that is
connected with the Rooster.

*Sorrowful
baby*

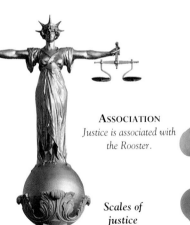

ASSOCIATION
Justice is associated with
the Rooster.

*Scales of
justice*

SINGING ROOSTER

~ 1945 2005 ~

In Chinese mythology, the Rooster is considered to be a very courageous creature. As a result, it is often carved on the tops of houses as a protection against evil spirits.

As the Singing Rooster, you are associated with success and expansion. Perhaps this is similar to the chest of a confident Rooster, which swells when the Rooster is singing, or feels proud.

PERSONALITY

You tend to be extremely outspoken and fearless, and your powers of articulation are immense. It is likely to be your sincere belief that you should talk about everything that you see and hear.

You invariably feel that what you consider to be wrong should be denounced, and that in the same way, what you consider to be right should be praised.

Although this honesty is very admirable, it is unlikely to make you many friends, or at least not at first. Because you set yourself high standards, and are always willing to speak out and make your views known, you tend to expect other people to do the same as a simple matter of course.

This natural idealism makes it very hard for you to suffer fools gladly. Perhaps you should try a little harder, for a little tolerance may make life considerably more pleasurable for you, as well as for those around you.

CAREER

Luckily, your forthright manner does not hinder success in your career in any way. You should find that life treats you well, and if you are sensible with money, you are likely to prosper.

FRIENDSHIPS

You are linked with blossoming. This is auspicious, for it represents longevity. Since you are likely to

Singing Rooster

enjoy long life, it is even more important for you to try and control your tendency to offend people – you are likely to need your friends for many years to come.

FAMILY
Your family has immense importance in your life. You are likely to have a good relationship with your parents, and should be able to get on well with your siblings, even though they may be in awe of you.

The essential value of a contented family life is fully appreciated by you, and you are always likely to do everything in your power to ensure that your family remains happy, peaceful, and stable.

Beware, however, of expecting too much from your children. Be generous, and try to give them the freedom to be themselves.

RELATIONSHIPS
Even though you may be slightly wild in your emotional affairs before you commit yourself, essentially you are a family person. Therefore, both your partner and your children should consider you to be a supportive and enjoyable companion.

LONELY ROOSTER

~ 1957 2017 ~

*This Rooster stands apart from the bustle of the farmyard,
but it is not a sad creature. Although it sometimes find life
a struggle, the Lonely Rooster is very caring.*

You are associated with a bee sting. Symbolically, this suggests that just as the bee that stings must suffer death, so you must suffer some loneliness while you pursue your sense of identity.

YOUTH

At school, you may have found it difficult to be part of a crowd. In the same way, during your early years at work, you invariably found the cut and thrust of a working life difficult to cope with. Most dynamic environments are likely to disturb you in your youth, because they are alien to your personality.

PERSONALITY

You have a caring and gentle personality, and are easily upset by aggressive behaviour. You need to be well liked and admired, and you also enjoy making other people happy.

Ironically, this desire to make everyone feel comfortable can put you at a disadvantage. This should change when you have greater control over situations, however.

You can be particularly liberal with your cash, and with your credit. Although this generosity comes naturally to you, it can sometimes turn into a hindrance, for bad debts may have a detrimental affect on your good friendships.

FRIENDSHIPS

Try to distinguish between the occasions when people are actually in need of your financial help, and the times when they require your spiritual or moral support.

Unfortunately, the unscrupulous might sometimes consider you to be very easily parted from your money. Perhaps it will prove most beneficial for you to remember that having a

Lonely Rooster

gentle and caring nature is not necessarily to be equated with being silly and sentimental.

PROSPECTS
As you grow older, people in influential positions should find that you are exactly the type of person they want to work with, and to have as a friend. This is likely to bring you many rewards.

Your prospects should be furthered, for you will be operating in a mature social circle. Here, you are likely to be fully appreciated for the person you are, and for the way in which you treat others.

Hopefully, you should find that the difficulties of your youth will be more than compensated for by the considerable advantages of middle age and beyond.

ROOSTER ANNOUNCING THE DAWN

~ 1909 1969 ~

This is the Rooster in its natural position — loudly heralding the glorious new day. It will announce the dawn whether or not anyone wishes to hear its song.

You are associated with a cutting instrument — something that does an efficient job, but that may also scythe things down.

PERSONALITY

You tend to say and do what you think is right, without worrying about the consequences. You are prone to go charging in, when caution might dictate otherwise.

Unfortunately, your behaviour sometimes upsets and disturbs people, but you feel that it is your duty to behave in this way.

However, you are very clever. Perhaps you should hold on to your sense of doing what is right, but also fuse it with your wisdom.

Once you allow yourself to admit it, you are, in fact, a very considerate person indeed. Try to allow this side of your personality to have more

dominance. As a result, other people should listen more carefully to whatever you have to say.

FAMILY

You are likely to have your children rather late in life. This is probably for the best, since your maturity should make you appreciate your children all the more.

It may take you many years to learn how to cope with the more difficult aspects of your personality. Consequently, you may find that you have estranged yourself from your parents and siblings.

Always be prepared to rebuild the bridges between you. Your parents and your siblings probably had to endure considerable aggravation from you in the past, therefore it is only fair for you to make an effort in your newly found maturity.

Rooster Announcing the Dawn

RELATIONSHIPS

It might take some time to find the right partner, but you should have a happy committed relationship.

PROSPECTS

You should enjoy a successful life, and a prosperous career. Take care with money, for you possess two conflicting trends within your personality. You have the capacity to be very careful with your money, or even mean, but you are also capable of suddenly deciding that you want to waste your money on the most unnecessary fripperies.

Make every effort to control this duality, for it could complicate your life. Enjoy your money by all means, but do not allow your extreme love of spending to deteriorate into uncontrolled binging.

ROOSTER IN THE CAGE

~ 1921 1981 ~

There are two powerful strands within this Rooster, which must be kept in harmony. It is associated with two hands that are trying to balance something.

This Rooster is likely to be well cared for, and well fed. It may even be treated as a pet, and should lead a very easy life.

Such a pampered lifestyle does have its disadvantages, however, for this Rooster may find that it is being fattened up for a future meal. Even if there are no immediate plans to eat this Rooster, its freedom to roam and forage is likely to be limited.

PERSONALITY

Essentially, there are two sides to your personality. Everything in life may seem to be going your way — you are likely to be successful, and to get what you want. People probably pay you lots of attention, and you are very clever. You are enjoyable company, and tend to be a natural performer. You like to show yourself off and dress well, and you tend to be able to hold your own in any

argument. Other people often find your skills and your knowledge highly impressive.

FAMILY

This is only half of your life story, however. The other half is that you may experience severe difficulties with your family. You may have disappointed them, and they could have problems in getting on with you. In this delicate family situation you are most likely to resemble a cooped up, frustrated Rooster.

RELATIONSHIPS

You may experience similar difficulties in your committed relationship. Perhaps your partner does not always respond to you with the enthusiasm or admiration that you might like. Bear in mind that this might be because you are being rather arrogant, even "cocky".

Rooster in the Cage

Although you are undoubtedly clever and highly accomplished, this does not necessarily mean that people have to lavish you with constant praise. It might be valuable for you to learn a little humility.

Once you have your arrogance under some sort of control, you should find that your life, successful as it is, will become even more enjoyable and fulfilling.

PROSPECTS

Throughout your life, you are often likely to experience a sense of being restricted, or of not being as fully appreciated as you might expect. Perhaps your expectations are unrealistic. Try not to expect too much from other people, and concentrate instead on the undeniable friendships and the many achievements that you have made.

ROOSTER IN THE HEN ROOST

~ 1933 1993 ~

*This could be seen as the ultimate location for the Rooster,
for in the Hen Roost, it should be fully appreciated.
Consequently, this is an auspicious sign.*

You are associated with doing what is right, and being able to enjoy the resulting good fortune.

PERSONALITY

You have a lively, vivacious personality. Even though you may always seem to be on the verge of trouble, somehow you manage to land on your feet. You may sometimes seem a little wild, but no one should mind your behaviour too much. You are frank, open, and likable. However, you have a tendency to gossip, which could alienate some people. You are fortunate, and tend to retain your friendships, even when you may have revealed a confidence.

CAREER

Progress in your career may not go smoothly, but you are never likely to find yourself in serious trouble. In a business partnership, you are likely to be absolutely convinced that you will do well. Unfortunately, your business partners might not share your confidence. Try to learn to operate at their pace, otherwise you might find their apparent slowness highly irritating.

FAMILY

Your family background may seem to be against your business interests, but as usual, you should be able to make a success of your situation. This might cause some resentment, but you are advised to be generous in your response.

RELATIONSHIPS

Your committed relationship is likely to be happy, even though the thoughtlessness of your actions could sometimes put it under great strain. Try to be more considerate, and do

Rooster in the Hen Roost

not always rely on your innate good fortune to see you through. Any sign of thoughtfulness and consideration from you is likely to ensure a happier committed relationship.

PROSPECTS

It is highly unlikely that you will ever find yourself short of financial resources. Although you always tend to spend much more lavishly than you should, good luck invariably comes to the rescue.

You should take care, however, for a sense of overconfidence could lead to disaster. Although you are a

naturally fortunate person, it might prove to be a costly mistake to push your luck too far.

The world is sometimes an unfair place, and since you are very fortunate, you should try to remember those who do not share your good fortune. Always give generously to those in need. It is likely that you will always have plenty, whereas many people have little, and no hope of change.

By learning to combine your good fortune with compassion, you should find that the quality of your life will be very high indeed.

YOUR CHINESE
MONTH OF BIRTH

Find the table with your year of birth, and see where your birthday falls. For example, if you were born on 30 August 1957, you were born in Chinese month 8

1 You are very skilful when dealing with difficult situations, and make other people feel relaxed.

2 You dislike other people's advice, and can be very hard in your approach. Try to listen more.

3 You are kindhearted, and assess situations well. Always try to keep your jealousy under control.

4 You are popular, an excellent organizer, and a good friend. You are also blessed with robust health.

5 You have enormous drive. You are very self-confident, but should also allow others to have their say.

6 You rarely give anything enough time or attention. Try to find a patient, helpful partner.

7 You are very efficient, and a good judge of character, but be prepared to revise your opinions.

8 You are rather weak, and upset people with your indifference. Try to moderate your behaviour.

9 You are a very charismatic individual, and a natural performer. Your life may not always be easy.

10 You are popular, successful, and make an excellent leader. You suffer in silence from poor health.

11 You can be extremely naive, yet you still sail through life, much to other people's amazement.

12 Your emotions will lead you into interesting situations, and your life should never be dull.

* Some Chinese years contain double months:	
1909: Month 2	1933: Month 5
22 Feb – 21 March	24 May – 22 June
22 March – 19 April	23 June – 21 July
1957: Month 8	1993: Month 3
25 Aug – 23 Sept	23 March – 21 April
24 Sept – 22 Oct	22 April – 20 May

1909	
22 Jan – 21 Feb	1
* See double months box	2
20 April – 18 May	3
19 May – 17 June	4
18 June – 16 July	5
17 July – 15 Aug	6
16 Aug – 13 Sept	7
14 Sept – 13 Oct	8
14 Oct – 12 Nov	9
13 Nov – 12 Dec	10
13 Dec – 10 Jan 1910	11
11 Jan – 9 Feb	12

1921	
8 Feb – 9 March	1
10 March – 7 April	2
8 April – 7 May	3
8 May – 5 June	4
6 June – 4 July	5
5 July – 3 Aug	6
4 Aug – 1 Sept	7
2 Sept – 30 Sept	8
1 Oct – 30 Oct	9
31 Oct – 28 Nov	10
29 Nov – 28 Dec	11
29 Dec – 27 Jan 1922	12

1933	
26 Jan – 23 Feb	1
24 Feb – 25 March	2
26 March – 24 April	3
25 April – 23 May	4
* See double months box	5
22 July – 20 Aug	6
21 Aug – 19 Sept	7
20 Sept – 18 Oct	8
19 Oct – 17 Nov	9
18 Nov – 16 Dec	10
17 Dec – 14 Jan 1934	11
15 Jan – 13 Feb	12

1945	
13 Feb – 13 March	1
14 March – 11 April	2
12 April – 11 May	3
12 May – 9 June	4
10 June – 8 July	5
9 July – 7 Aug	6
8 Aug – 5 Sept	7
6 Sept – 5 Oct	8
6 Oct – 4 Nov	9
5 Nov – 4 Dec	10
5 Dec – 2 Jan 1946	11
3 Jan – 1 Feb	12

1957	
31 Jan – 1 March	1
2 March – 30 March	2
31 March – 29 April	3
30 April – 28 May	4
29 May – 27 June	5
28 June – 26 July	6
27 July – 24 Aug	7
* See double months box	8
23 Oct – 21 Nov	9
22 Nov – 20 Dec	10
21 Dec – 19 Jan 1958	11
20 Jan – 17 Feb	12

1969	
17 Feb – 17 March	1
18 March – 16 April	2
17 April – 15 May	3
16 May – 14 June	4
15 June – 13 July	5
14 July – 12 Aug	6
13 Aug – 11 Sept	7
12 Sept – 10 Oct	8
11 Oct – 9 Nov	9
10 Nov – 8 Dec	10
9 Dec – 7 Jan 1970	11
8 Jan – 5 Feb	12

1981	
5 Feb – 5 March	1
6 March – 4 April	2
5 April – 3 May	3
4 May – 1 June	4
2 June – 1 July	5
2 July – 30 July	6
31 July – 28 Aug	7
29 Aug – 27 Sept	8
28 Sept – 27 Oct	9
28 Oct – 25 Nov	10
26 Nov – 25 Dec	11
26 Dec – 24 Jan 1982	12

1993	
23 Jan – 20 Feb	1
21 Feb – 22 March	2
* See double months box	3
21 May – 19 June	4
20 June – 18 July	5
19 July – 17 Aug	6
18 Aug – 15 Sept	7
16 Sept – 14 Oct	8
15 Oct – 13 Nov	9
14 Nov – 12 Dec	10
13 Dec – 11 Jan 1994	11
12 Jan – 9 Feb	12

2005	
9 Feb – 9 March	1
10 March – 8 April	2
9 April – 7 May	3
8 May – 6 June	4
7 June – 5 July	5
6 July – 7 Aug	6
8 Aug – 3 Sept	7
4 Sept – 2 Oct	8
3 Oct – 1 Nov	9
2 Nov – 30 Nov	10
1 Dec – 30 Dec	11
31 Dec – 28 Jan 2006	12

YOUR CHINESE
DAY OF BIRTH

*Refer to the previous page to discover the beginning of your
Chinese month of birth, then use the chart below to
calculate your Chinese day of birth.*

If you were born on 5 May 1909,
your birthday is in the month starting
on 20 April. Find 20 on the chart
below. Using 20 as the first day,
count the days until you reach the
date of your birthday. Remember
that not all months contain 31 days.
You were born on day 16 of the
Chinese month.

  If you were born in a Chinese
double month, simply count the days
from the first date of the month that
contains your birthday.

1	2	3	4	5	6	7
8	9	10	11	12	13	14
15	16	17	18	19	20	21
22	23	24	25	26	27	28
29	30	31				

DAY 1, 10, 19, OR 28
You are trustworthy, and set high
standards, but tend to rush your

projects. Try to be cautious, and do
not be too self-obsessed. You may
receive unexpected money, but must
control your spending. You are
suited to a career in the public sector
or the arts.

DAY 2, 11, 20, OR 29
You are honest and popular. You
need peace, but also require lively
company. You are prone to
outbursts of temper. You tend to
enjoy life, and make the most of your
opportunities. You are suited to a
literary or artistic career.

DAY 3, 12, 21, OR 30
You are quick-witted, but may
appear to be difficult. As a result,
people may be wary of being your
friend. You have a disciplined
character, and fight for the truth.
You are suited to careers that have a
competitive element.

Day 4, 13, 22, or 31

You are very warmhearted, but also have a reserved attitude, which can sometimes make you appear unapproachable. If you try to be more outgoing and sociable, you should become more popular. You have a calm and patient manner, and are suited to a career as an academic or a researcher.

Day 5, 14, or 23

Your fiery, obstinate nature can sometimes make it difficult for you to accept suggestions or opinions from others, and your stubbornness may lead to quarrels or problems. You should be lucky with money, and may often use your profits to set up new projects. Your innate intelligence will enable you to cope with a demanding career.

Day 6, 15, or 24

You have an open, stable, and cheerful character, and enjoy an active social life. You are affectionate and emotional, and have a tendency to daydream. This can lead to confusion, and your eagerness to help others may be stifled by your indecision. Although you will never be wealthy, you should always have enough money.

Day 7, 16, or 25

You enjoy a certain amount of excitement in your life, but must learn to become more realistic and disciplined. Although you are a natural performer, you should beware of alienating your friends or colleagues. In your career, the opportunity to travel is more important to you than a good salary or a high standard of living.

Day 8, 17, or 26

You have good judgement, but should not act too quickly. Your social skills may sometimes be lacking, and you may alienate other people, so try to be more tactful. You will experience poverty, but also wealth. Your calm and determined nature is combined with a free spirit, making you best suited to self-employment.

Day 9, 18, or 27

You are happy, optimistic, and warmhearted. You keep yourself busy, and are rarely troubled by trivialities. Occasionally you quarrel unnecessarily with your friends, and it is important for you to learn to control your moods. You are particularly suited to a career as a sole director or proprietor.

YOUR CHINESE
HOUR OF BIRTH

In Chinese time, one hour is equal to two Western hours.
Each Chinese double hour is associated with one of the
twelve astrological animals.

11 P.M. – 1 A.M. RAT HOUR
You are independent and have a hot temper. Try to think before you speak. Your thrifty nature will be useful in business and at home. You are always willing to help those who are close to you, and they will return your support.

1 – 3 A.M. OX HOUR
Up to the age of twenty, your life could be difficult, but your fortunes are likely to improve after these troublesome years. In your career, be prepared to take a risk or to leave home during your youth to achieve your goals. You should enjoy a prosperous old age.

3 – 5 A.M. TIGER HOUR
You have a lively and creative nature, which may cause family arguments in your youth. Between the ages of twenty and forty you may have many problems. Luckily, your fortunes are likely to improve dramatically in your forties.

5 – 7 A.M. RABBIT HOUR
Your parents should be helpful, but your siblings may be your rivals. You may have to move away from home to achieve your full potential at work. Your committed relationship may take time to become settled, but you should get along much better with everyone after middle age.

7 – 9 A.M. DRAGON HOUR
You have a quick-witted, determined, and attractive nature. Your life will be busy, but you could sometimes be lonely. You should achieve a good standard of living. Try to curb your excessive self-confidence, for it could make working relationships difficult.

9 – 11 A.M. SNAKE HOUR

You have a talent for business and should find it easy to build your career and provide for your family. You have a particularly generous spirit, and will gladly help your friends when they are in trouble. Unfortunately, family relationships are unlikely to run smoothly.

11 A.M. – 1 P.M. HORSE HOUR

You are active, clever, and obstinate. Try to listen to advice. You are fascinated with travel and with changing your life. Learn to control your extravagance, for it could lead to financial suffering.

1 – 3 P.M. RAM HOUR

Steady relationships with your family, friends, or partners are difficult, because you have an active nature. You are clever, but must not force your views on others. Your fortunes are likely to be at their lowest in your middle age.

3 – 5 P.M. MONKEY HOUR

You earn and spend money easily. Your character is attractive, but frustrating, too. Sometimes your parents are not able to give you adequate moral support. Your committed relationship should be good, but do not brood over emotional problems for too long – if you do your career could suffer.

5 – 7 P.M. ROOSTER HOUR

In your teenage years you may have many arguments with your family. There could even be a family division, which should eventually be resolved. You are trustworthy, kind, and warmhearted, and never intend to hurt other people.

7 – 9 P.M. DOG HOUR

Your brave, capable, hard-working nature is ideally suited to self-employment, and the forecast for your career is excellent. Try to control your impatience and vanity. The quality of your life is far more important to you than the amount of money you have saved.

9 – 11 P.M. PIG HOUR

You are particularly skilled at manual work and always set yourself the highest of standards. Although you are warmhearted, you do not like to surround yourself with too many friends. However, the people who are close to you have your complete trust. You can be easily upset by others, but are able to forgive and forget quickly.

YOUR FORTUNE IN OTHER ANIMAL YEARS

The Rooster's fortunes fluctuate during the twelve animal years. It is best to concentrate on a year's positive aspects, and to take care when faced with the seemingly negative.

YEAR OF THE RAT
Your family life is highly auspicious in the Year of the Rat. A sense of happiness will be the common thread that links you with your relatives. There are likely to be many opportunities to celebrate the family's good fortune.

YEAR OF THE OX
You have the potential for success in the Year of the Ox. Unfortunately, there is a price to pay, in the form of hard work and struggle. Quarrels and disagreements could sap your energy, therefore you should do your best to avoid them.

YEAR OF THE TIGER
This is an excellent year for your professional life, and you should make great progress. If you are self-employed your business will flourish, and if you are an employee you are likely to be promoted swiftly.

YEAR OF THE RABBIT
Financial success is likely to be yours in the Year of the Rabbit. However, you must make every effort to restrain your profligate streak. If you allow it too much freedom, your financial rewards could diminish or even disappear entirely.

YEAR OF THE DRAGON
This is potentially a very good year for the Rooster. The Year of the Dragon should bring you considerable success and happiness, and there is also a strong possibility that you could find yourself enjoying some fame and renown.

YEAR OF THE SNAKE
Your professional life is auspicious in the Year of the Snake, and you are likely to be promoted. However, be prepared for disappointment when your increased responsibilities do not necessarily correspond to increased financial rewards.

YEAR OF THE HORSE
It is important that you keep yourself under control in the Year of the Horse. It will be a demanding year in various areas of your life. However, do not give in to anger, frustration, or resentment, for you will only make matters worse.

YEAR OF THE RAM
In general, the Year of the Ram is a good year for the Rooster. However, as well as enjoying a degree of success, you are also likely to find yourself responding to an underlying sadness or a sense of melancholy within your family.

YEAR OF THE MONKEY
At times, it may seem as if nothing is going right for you in the Year of the Monkey. Seemingly never-ending difficulties will depress and exhaust you, but try not to give in to despair, because this will invariably make matters worse.

YEAR OF THE ROOSTER
After the difficulties of last year, your own year can only be a marked improvement. Although you will be confronted by many problems throughout the year, you should be able to overcome them with ease.

YEAR OF THE DOG
Your fortune is mixed during the Year of the Dog. You should enjoy success at work, and happiness in your family life. However, you may have to travel too often and too widely, and there could be difficulties ahead.

YEAR OF THE PIG
It is important that you take good care of yourself in the Year of the Pig, because you are particularly susceptible to ill-health. Try to be cautious and vigilant, and watch out for potential accidents or troublesome incidents.

YOUR CHINESE
YEAR OF BIRTH

Your astrological animal corresponds to the Chinese year of your birth. It is the single most important key in the quest to unlock your Chinese horoscope.

Find your Western year of birth in the left-hand column of the chart. Your Chinese astrological animal is on the same line as your year of birth, in the right-hand column of the chart. If you were born in the beginning of the year, check the middle column of the chart carefully. For example, if you were born in 1970, you might assume that you belong to the Year of the Dog. However, if your birthday falls before 6 February, you actually belong to the Year of the Rooster.

1900	31 Jan – 18 Feb 1901	Rat
1901	19 Feb – 7 Feb 1902	Ox
1902	8 Feb – 28 Jan 1903	Tiger
1903	29 Jan – 15 Feb 1904	Rabbit
1904	16 Feb – 3 Feb 1905	Dragon
1905	4 Feb – 24 Jan 1906	Snake
1906	25 Jan – 12 Feb 1907	Horse
1907	13 Feb – 1 Feb 1908	Ram
1908	2 Feb – 21 Jan 1909	Monkey
1909	22 Jan – 9 Feb 1910	Rooster
1910	10 Feb – 29 Jan 1911	Dog
1911	30 Jan – 17 Feb 1912	Pig
1912	18 Feb – 5 Feb 1913	Rat
1913	6 Feb – 25 Jan 1914	Ox
1914	26 Jan – 13 Feb 1915	Tiger
1915	14 Feb – 2 Feb 1916	Rabbit
1916	3 Feb – 22 Jan 1917	Dragon

1917	23 Jan – 10 Feb 1918	Snake
1918	11 Feb – 31 Jan 1919	Horse
1919	1 Feb – 19 Feb 1920	Ram
1920	20 Feb – 7 Feb 1921	Monkey
1921	8 Feb – 27 Jan 1922	Rooster
1922	28 Jan – 15 Feb 1923	Dog
1923	16 Feb – 4 Feb 1924	Pig
1924	5 Feb – 23 Jan 1925	Rat
1925	24 Jan – 12 Feb 1926	Ox
1926	13 Feb – 1 Feb 1927	Tiger
1927	2 Feb – 22 Jan 1928	Rabbit
1928	23 Jan – 9 Feb 1929	Dragon
1929	10 Feb – 29 Jan 1930	Snake
1930	30 Jan – 16 Feb 1931	Horse
1931	17 Feb – 5 Feb 1932	Ram
1932	6 Feb – 25 Jan 1933	Monkey
1933	26 Jan – 13 Feb 1934	Rooster

1934	14 Feb – 3 Feb 1935	Dog	1971	27 Jan – 14 Feb 1972	Pig
1935	4 Feb – 23 Jan 1936	Pig	1972	15 Feb – 2 Feb 1973	Rat
1936	24 Jan – 10 Feb 1937	Rat	1973	3 Feb – 22 Jan 1974	Ox
1937	11 Feb – 30 Jan 1938	Ox	1974	23 Jan – 10 Feb 1975	Tiger
1938	31 Jan – 18 Feb 1939	Tiger	1975	11 Feb – 30 Jan 1976	Rabbit
1939	19 Feb – 7 Feb 1940	Rabbit	1976	31 Jan – 17 Feb 1977	Dragon
1940	8 Feb – 26 Jan 1941	Dragon	1977	18 Feb – 6 Feb 1978	Snake
1941	27 Jan – 14 Feb 1942	Snake	1978	7 Feb – 27 Jan 1979	Horse
1942	15 Feb – 4 Feb 1943	Horse	1979	28 Jan – 15 Feb 1980	Ram
1943	5 Feb – 24 Jan 1944	Ram	1980	16 Feb – 4 Feb 1981	Monkey
1944	25 Jan – 12 Feb 1945	Monkey	1981	5 Feb – 24 Jan 1982	Rooster
1945	13 Feb – 1 Feb 1946	Rooster	1982	25 Jan – 12 Feb 1983	Dog
1946	2 Feb – 21 Jan 1947	Dog	1983	13 Feb – 1 Feb 1984	Pig
1947	22 Jan – 9 Feb 1948	Pig	1984	2 Feb – 19 Feb 1985	Rat
1948	10 Feb – 28 Jan 1949	Rat	1985	20 Feb – 8 Feb 1986	Ox
1949	29 Jan – 16 Feb 1950	Ox	1986	9 Feb – 28 Jan 1987	Tiger
1950	17 Feb – 5 Feb 1951	Tiger	1987	29 Jan – 16 Feb 1988	Rabbit
1951	6 Feb – 26 Jan 1952	Rabbit	1988	17 Feb – 5 Feb 1989	Dragon
1952	27 Jan – 13 Feb 1953	Dragon	1989	6 Feb – 26 Jan 1990	Snake
1953	14 Feb – 2 Feb 1954	Snake	1990	27 Jan – 14 Feb 1991	Horse
1954	3 Feb – 23 Jan 1955	Horse	1991	15 Feb – 3 Feb 1992	Ram
1955	24 Jan – 11 Feb 1956	Ram	1992	4 Feb – 22 Jan 1993	Monkey
1956	12 Feb – 30 Jan 1957	Monkey	1993	23 Jan – 9 Feb 1994	Rooster
1957	31 Jan – 17 Feb 1958	Rooster	1994	10 Feb – 30 Jan 1995	Dog
1958	18 Feb – 7 Feb 1959	Dog	1995	31 Jan – 18 Feb 1996	Pig
1959	8 Feb – 27 Jan 1960	Pig	1996	19 Feb – 6 Feb 1997	Rat
1960	28 Jan – 14 Feb 1961	Rat	1997	7 Feb – 27 Jan 1998	Ox
1961	15 Feb – 4 Feb 1962	Ox	1998	28 Jan – 15 Feb 1999	Tiger
1962	5 Feb – 24 Jan 1963	Tiger	1999	16 Feb – 4 Feb 2000	Rabbit
1963	25 Jan – 12 Feb 1964	Rabbit	2000	5 Feb – 23 Jan 2001	Dragon
1964	13 Feb – 1 Feb 1965	Dragon	2001	24 Jan – 11 Feb 2002	Snake
1965	2 Feb – 20 Jan 1966	Snake	2002	12 Feb – 31 Jan 2003	Horse
1966	21 Jan – 8 Feb 1967	Horse	2003	1 Feb – 21 Jan 2004	Ram
1967	9 Feb – 29 Jan 1968	Ram	2004	22 Jan – 8 Feb 2005	Monkey
1968	30 Jan – 16 Feb 1969	Monkey	2005	9 Feb – 28 Jan 2006	Rooster
1969	17 Feb – 5 Feb 1970	Rooster	2006	29 Jan – 17 Feb 2007	Dog
1970	6 Feb – 26 Jan 1971	Dog	2007	18 Feb – 6 Feb 2008	Pig